QUESTIONS
AND
REPLIES

A
MILITARY
CLASSIC
FROM
ANCIENT
CHINA

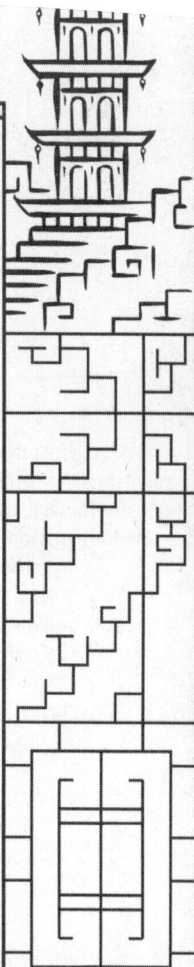

Cherry Stone Publishing, an imprint of
Sweet Cherry Publishing Limited
Unit 36, Vulcan House,
Vulcan Road,
Leicester, LE5 3EF
United Kingdom

First published by Cherry Stone Publishing in 2021
2021 edition

2 4 6 8 10 9 7 5 3 1

ISBN: 978-1-78226-967-0

© Sweet Cherry Publishing

Questions and Replies

All rights reserved. No part of this publication may be
reproduced or utilised in any form or by any means, electronic
or mechanical, including photocopying, recording, or using
any information storage and retrieval system, without prior
permission in writing from the publisher.

This book is copyright under the Berne Convention.
No reproduction without permission.
All rights reserved.

Cover design and illustrations
by Sophie Jones

www.cherrystonepublishing.com

Printed and bound in India
I.TP002

QUESTIONS AND REPLIES

BETWEEN EMPEROR TAIZONG OF TANG AND GENERAL LI JING

CHERRY STONE
PUBLISHING

CHAPTER I.

VOLUME I

1

Emperor Taizong asked: "Goryeo has invaded Silla several times and I sent an envoy to order the troops to stop. But Goryeo did not obey the edict, and I want to send troops to crush them. What do you think?"

2

Li Jing replied: "According to the investigation, Yeon Gaesomun thinks that he is proficient in military affairs and that China is incapable of crushing him, so he dares to disobey your order. Please give me thirty thousand soldiers to capture him. Emperor Taizong asked: "With such a small number of troops and such a long distance, what method should be used against him?"

3

Li Jing replied: "With regular armed forces."

4

Emperor Taizong asked: "When you cracked down on the Turks, ad-hoc troops were the key to win, but now you propose to use the regular forces against Goryeo. What is the reason?"

5

Li Jing replied: "Zuge Liang captured Meng Huo seven times; he succeeded by using no other methods but regular forces."

6

Emperor Taizong asked: "When the Jin general Ma Long seized Liangzhou, he also followed Zhuge Liang's eightfold formation with chariots. In the open terrain, he put daggers and halberds in front of chariots, which resembled antlers; in the narrow road, he set up wooden huts on the chariots to advance and fight at the same time. There is no doubt that the use of regular soldiers was valued by the ancients!"

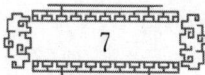

7

Li Jing replied: "When I crusaded against the Turks, I marched thousands of *li** to the west.

8

If I had marched without regular forces, how could I manage to engage in such a long expedition? Ma Long's use of chariots and antler-shaped arrangement were crucial strategies.

9

They helped maintain combat power, resist the enemy, and restrain his own troops.

10

As these three strengths were combined, they gave full play to the combat power. General Ma Long was skilled at this ancient strategy!"

*li is a traditional Chinese unit of distance that is about one third of a mile.

11

Emperor Taizong asked: "In the battle of Huoyi where we defeated Song Laosheng, our army retreated slightly at the beginning of the battle. At that time I led my elite cavalry to march down from Nanyuan and flanked the enemy, cutting off the retreat routes of Song Laosheng's army, trouncing them, and capturing Song Laosheng alive. Is this a use of regular forces or ad-hoc forces?"

12

Li Jing replied: "Your Majesty's wisdom and strategy is a gift that cannot be learned by ordinary people.

13

According to the theories on the art of war, since the Yellow Emperor, the strategy of using the army is always to send the regular forces first before deploying ad-hoc troops to win; one shall first use benevolence and righteousness, and then authority and deception.

14

In the battle of Huoyi, our army was sent because of righteousness, which made it a just army.

15

After Li Jiancheng the commander fell off his horse, the right army retreated slightly, which was a use of ad-hoc strategy."

16

Emperor Taizong asked: "The retreat at the time almost ruined everything. What do you mean by ad-hoc strategy?"

17

Li Jing replied: "In warfare, regular forces are ordered to attack forward and ad-hoc forces are ordered to retreat.

18

If the right army at the time had not not retreated, how could it lure Laosheng to attack with full force? According to Sun Tzu's Art of War: 'Lure the enemy with a small advantage, take advantage of his confusion and then attack.' Laosheng did not know the art of war, and relied solely on his courage to charge.

19

He was unexpectedly cut off from the back by Your Majesty and captured by you. This is when the use of ad-hoc forces contributed to the use of main forces."

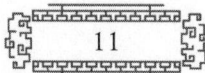

20

Emperor Taizong asked: "The distinguished General Huo Qubing practised strategies that were consistent with the Art of War proposed by Sun Tzu and Wu Zi.

21

Is that true? When our right army retreated slightly at the time, the Emperor Gaozu was terrified and I took the opportunity to attack from the side and rear, which instead resulted in the victory of our army.

22

This strategy is also in line with what Sun Tzu and Wu Zi advocated. Your words are indeed insightful."

23

Emperor Taizong asked: "So is it true that any retreating forces are a use of ad-hoc strategy?"

24

Li Jing replied: "Not necessarily." When the army retreats, if the banners are unevenly distributed; if the drumbeats are not in harmony and the orders are noisy and not unified, then the retreat signals failure instead of ad-hoc strategy.

25

If the banners are neat and tidy; if the drumbeats are in harmony and the orders are unified; if the men and horses seem chaotic but still maintain formations, then the retreat does not lead to defeat, but the use of ad-hoc strategy.

26

According to Sun Tzu's the Art of War: if the enemy 'pretends to be defeated, do not pursue.' 'You can fight but pretend not to be able to fight.' This is the wise use of ad-hoc forces."

27

Emepror Taizong asked: "Was it the will of heaven that the right army retreated slightly in the battle of Huoyi? Was the capture of Song Laosheng the result of human effort?"

28

Li Jing replied: "If it was not for the fact that Your Majesty succeeded in the interactions of regular and ad-hoc forces, how could we have won? Therefore the use of regular and ad-hoc forces is a matter of decision for a brilliant strategist.

29

Their interactions can be mysterious and unpredictable; therefore people often attribute it to the will of heaven."
Emperor Taizong agreed.

30

Emperor Taizong asked: "Is the difference between the regular and ad-hoc forces made beforehand, or is it a decision based on different situations?"

31

Li Jing replied: "According to the Art of War commentary by Cao Cao: 'If I have twice the size of enemy troops, I will divide my troops into two, with one part as the regular forces and the other as the ad-hoc forces; if I have five times the size of enemy troops, I will take three fifths as the regular forces and the rest as the ad-hoc forces.' This is only a general statement.

32

As Sun Tzu put it: 'The types of warfare lie in nothing but the use of regular and ad-hoc forces.

33

There is no end to the variations of the two.

34

They can be converted into each other like a spinning circle with infinite mysteries.' This is the true nature of them.

35

How can you distinguish between the two beforehand? If soldiers have not learned the battle techniques and the commanders are not familiar with the orders, it is necessary to distinguish between the regular and ad-hoc troops to train them.

36

During drills, each unit should recognise the banners and drums of the commanders, and repeatedly practice changes of formations according to the commanders.

37

This is the way to train.

38

When the training is completed and the soldiers are familiar with the strategies, then they can be commanded like sheep and goats by the general.

39

Who would recognise the difference between regular and ad-hoc forces then! This is what Sun Tzu called 'Use all kinds of deceptions to confuse the enemy, so that they never know my real plan'.

40

This is the ultimate deployment of regular and ad-hoc tactics.

41

Therefore, the distinction between the two is usually made for training purposes, while there is no end to their variations during war."

42

Emperor Taizong said: "The use of these strategies is so profound!" Cao Cao must be a master strategist. However, his book only teaches general rules to commanders, not specifically the art of regular and ad-hoc tactics."

43

Emperor Taizong said: "Cao Cao proposed that 'ad-hoc forces shall strike the enemy from the side'. What do you think?"

44

Li Jing replied: "When Cao commented on Sun Tzu's Art of War, he said: 'The first to engage the enemy are the regular forces, and the later to surprise the enemy are the ad-hoc forces.' He did not mention the attack from the side. As far as I am concerned, he argued that the forces that engage the enemy at front are the regular forces, and the forces that seize the opportunity to win by surprise are the ad-hoc forces.

45

How can we be rigid when it comes to when and where the two forces shall be deployed?

46

Emperor Taizong said: "So my regular soldiers were considered ad-hoc ones by the enemy; and my ad-hoc soldiers were taken as regular forces by the enemy.

47

This is what Sun Tzu referred to as 'deception', right? The regular forces turned into ad-hoc ones and vice versa.

48

These unpredictable changes are what Sun Tzu referred to as 'clueless to track', right?"

49

Li Jing bowed again and said: "Your Majesty, your words are far beyond the wisdom of the ancestors and beyond my reach."

50

Emperor Taizong said: "As the army separates and gathers, how can regular and ad-hoc troops deployed?"

51

Li Jing replied: "Brilliant strategists deploy regular and ad-hoc troops all the time; it is too unpredictable for the enemy to tell. They win no matter which forces they deploy.
Even their soldiers do not get the reason of the victory.
Only those who master the art of these two strategies can achieve this! Only Sun Tzu succeeded in the use of the two strategies as soldiers separated and gathered.
Wu Zi and others were no match for him."

52

Emperor Taizong asked: "What about Wu Zi's Art of War?"

53

Li Jing replied: "Please allow me to explain in a concise way.

54

Marquis Wu of Wei asked Wu Zi about how to perceive the talents of the enemy general.

55

Wu Zi replied: 'Send a brave subordinate officer to lead his troops to attack and retreat as soon as the two sides meet, and do not stop the retreat so as to observe the moves of the enemy.

56

If the enemy are restrained in advancing and halting, and do not pursue retreating troops, this is a sign of the enemy general's wisdom and strategy.

57

If the whole enemy army pursue and their soldiers move in disorder, this is a sign that the enemy general has no talent; attack them immediately without hesitation.' As far as I am concerned, Wu Zi's methods are mostly of this kind, which is different from Sun Tzu's approach of combining regular and ad-hoc forces."

58

Emperor Taizong asked: "Your uncle Han Qinwu once said that you can talk to him about Sun Tzu and Wu Zi's Art of War. Did he refer to the use of regular and ad-hoc forces?"

59

Li Jing replied: "What did he know about the essence of regular and ad-hoc strategies? He thought the regular stayed regular and the ad-hoc stayed ad-hoc.

60

But he never understood that they can be converted into each other as in an endless cycle."

61

Emperor Taizong asked: "In antiquity, people changed tactics right before war and attacked by surprise. Does it have anything to do with the art of regular and ad-hoc strategies?"

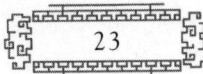

62

Li Jing replied: "In ancient battles, most of them were fought by people who had limited wisdom and tactics to defeat those who had neither, and by people who had limited ability to defeat those who were incompetent. What did they know about the art of war? For example, in the Eastern Jin Dynasty, Xie Xuan defeated Fu Jian not because Xie was a competent commander, but because Fu was an incompetent one."

63

Emperor Taizong asked his minister to take out Xie Xuan's Biography for his review.

64

Then he asked: "What did Fu Jian fail to do?"

65

Li Jing replied: "I read the Stories of Fu Jian, all the Qin armies were defeated at the time except Murong Chui's.

66

Fu Jian led the remnants of his army to Murong Chui's camp, and Murong Chui's son Murong Bao advised his father to kill Fu, but he did not.

67

From the situation that the Qin armies were defeated and Murong Chui's army alone remained intact, it is obvious that Fu Jian was framed by Murong Chui.

68

Then how could it be not difficult for Fu to win? That is why I think people like Fu Jian are incompetent."

69

Emperor Taizong asked: "Sun Tzu claimed in his Art of War that those who plan more can overcome those who plan less, so it seems that those who plan less can overcome those who do not at all. And this is true for everything."

70

Emperor Taizong said: "What is the name of the Yellow Emperor's book on the art of war? Is it Grasping Tactics or Grasping Opportunities?"

71

Li Jing replied: "The pronunciation of tactics can be read as the same with that of opportunities. That is why some change the title of tactics to opportunities. The meaning stays the same.

72

According to the book: 'The four regular formations are heaven, earth, wind and cloud; and the four ad-hoc tactics are dragon, tiger, bird and snake.

73

When the ad-hoc tactics are mastered by the general, this practice is called grasping tactics.' Ad-hoc tactics here refer to the use of remaining armed forces.

74

The pronunciation of tactics is the same as that of opportunities. As far as I am concerned, opportunities are ubiquitous in the art of war.

75

How can we only stick to the grasping of those opportunities? It is supposed to be the grasping of all the resources at disposal.

76

The use of regular forces is ordered by the monarch, while the use of ad-hoc forces is determined by the general.

77

According to Sun Tzu's Art of War: 'If the decrees of the state are carried out and the people are educated, the people will obey.' This is why the head of state is in charge of regular forces.

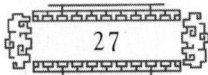

78

It also noted that: 'The orders of the monarch may be disregarded if they are not adapted to the situation on the battlefield.' This is why the general is in charge of ad-hoc forces.

79

A general who only knows how to use regular forces but not ad-hoc forces is a general who sticks blindly to the rules; a general who only knows how to use ad-hoc forces but not regular forces is a general who engages in recklessness; a general who uses both forces properly is a qualified general who can assist the state.

80

Therefore, there are no differences between grasping opportunities and grasping tactics.

81

The key is to be able to integrate the two."

82

Emperor Taizong asked: "It is said that Zhuge Liang's Eightfold Battle Formation is divided into nine parts; the extra one part in the centre is occupied by the general, and the surrounding eight formations are subject to his orders.

83

There are many small formations included in the big formation, and many small squads included in the big squad.

84

The front formation can be used as the rear formation and the rear formation as the front formation.

85

Once the enemy enter this formation, they cannot quickly attack the general in the centre, and it is very difficult for them to exit this formation, and are therefore caught in a dilemma.

86

The whole formation has four rear parts and eight front parts.

87

Whichever part that is attacked will immediately become the front part of the formation to meet the enemy.

88

If the enemy rush straight to the centre of the general, then both the front and rear parts of the formation can come to the rescue.

89

The predecessor of the eightfold formation was fivefold, but later Zhuge Liang transformed it into eightfold. Why is this?"

90

Li Jing replied: "Zhuge Liang used stones to arrange eight rows; the method of eightfold formation is similar to what the book Grasping Opportunities stated. I used to train formations and teach this eightfold formation first. Instructions about this formation from Grasping Opportunities are quite simple and general."

91

Emperor Taizong asked: "The names of the eightfold formation are: Heaven, Earth, Wind, Cloud, Dragon, Tiger, Bird and Snake. What do they mean?"

92

Li Jing replied: "The later generations misunderstood the names.

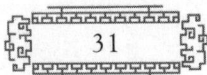

93

In order to keep the secret of this formation, the ancients deliberately gave it eight mysterious names.

94

Although the formation is eightfold, the eight parts act as a whole.

95

For example, Heaven and Earth were originally names for flags; Wind and Cloud names for banners; and Dragon, Tiger, Bird and Snake names for different units of troops.

96

Later generations did not know the ancient trickery. They misunderstood the eightfold formation and kept naming all kinds of big and small formation as well.

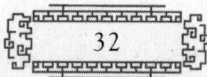

97

Now a lot more than eight formations bear their names, don't they?"

98

Emperor Taizong asked: "The eightfold formation was initially five, and eventually Zhuge Liang changed it into eight. It has nothing to do with giving names themselves; it is an ancient practice. Would you elaborate?"

99

Li Jing replied: "The Yellow Emperor first created the method of land ownership and established the military system based on the nine-square land distribution.

100

Four intersecting demarcation lines divided the army into eight squares with another square in the centre to divide land into nine squares in total.

101

Since the four corners in the Southeast, Southwest, Northwest and Northeast were free land, this is the origin of fivefold formation that was later converted into eightfold formation.

102

The central square was emptied for the general, with land in the front, in the back, on the right, on the left and in four corners connected together for an eightfold formation.

103

As the formation changed to fight the enemy, the troops would move frequently and wave flags.

104

Although the movement would be seemingly chaotic, in fact the formation remained in order.

105

They killed while running but the formation was maintained.

106

When they moved in a scattered way, the formation became eightfold; when they gathered, they united as one large formation."

107

Emperor Taizong said: "The Yellow Emperor was brilliant in his art of war!" Although the descendants had profound wisdom and strategy, no one was able to surpass his tactics. Who has inherited his art of war?"

108

Li Jing replied: "When the Western Zhou Dynasty was just emerging, Jiang Taigong compiled and revised the art of war of the Yellow Emperor and started to establish the nine-square land system in its capital.

109

He had three hundred chariots and three thousand warriors and created the military system of the Zhou Dynasty.

110

He established the combat method of marching troops.

111

In the battle of Muye, Jiang Taigong stormed the enemy with a vanguard of one hundred warriors and achieved a glorious victory over Shang's seven-hundred-thousand-strong army with forty-five thousand men.

112

The Methods of the Sima in the Zhou Dynasty was based on the Art of War of Taigong.

113

After the death of Taigong, the people of Qi inherited the Art of War from him.

114

By the time Duke Huan of Qi came to dominate the world, he had appointed Guan Zhong as the prime minister to compile the Art of War by Taigong.

115

The army of Qi was known as a well-disciplined and well-trained army.

116

All the vassal states were fearful and subservient at that time."

117

Emperor Taizong asked: "Most Confucianists think that Guan Zhong was just a strategist who ruled the world by hegemony, but I don't know that his art of war was actually based on the rule of kings.

118

Zhuge Liang was a wise man who assisted the emperor, and he often compared himself to Guan Zhong and Yue Yi, so we can see that Guan Zhong was also a wise advisor to the king.

119

Only at that time the king of Zhou was already in decline and he could not appoint Guan Zhong anymore, so he had to turn to the power of Qi to launch a war and conquer the world."

120

Li Jing replied: "Your Majesty are so wise and know people so thoroughly that even if I were to die now, I would still live up to the teachings of the sages.

121

Allow me to say a few words about the way Guan Zhong governed the state of Qi.

122

He divided the people of Qi into three parts and established three armies.

123

Administratively, five families formed a unit, and each family contributed one soldier for the unit of five.

124

Ten units of five formed a section of fifty men; four sections of fifty formed a company of two hundred men; ten companies formed a brigade of two thousand men; five brigades formed an army of ten thousand men.

125

According to the Methods of the Sima, an army was divided into five brigades and one brigade divided into five companies.

126

This approach was inherited from Taigong."

127

Emperor Taizong asked: "It is said that the Methods of the Sima was written by Sima Rangju. Is it true?"

128

Li Jing replied: "According to the Historical Biography of Sima Rangju, during the reign of Duke Jing of Qi, Tian Rangju was good at art of war and he had defeated the armies of Yan and Jin.

129

To award his outstanding service, Duke Jing appointed him as a Sima (meaning marshal in Chinese).

130

That is why people called him Sima Rangju and his descendants also took Sima as their family name.

131

King Wei of Qi studied the ancient art of war the Sima Rangju's military theories.

132

Then a few dozens of articles were compiled as the Methods of the Sima.

133

Nowadays, military science is divided into four methods: military power and strategy, military situation, military yin and yang, and military skills, which are all based on the ancient Sima method."

134

Emperor Taizong asked: "It is said that 'Zhang Liang and Han Xin from the Han Dynasty put the ancient art of war into one hundred and eighty-two different schools of thought. After screening, they deleted the fake and kept the essence that are thirty-five.' But now all of the thirty-five are lost. Why is that?"

135

Li Jing replied: "Zhang Liang studied Taigong's Six Secret Teachings and Three Strategies." Han Xin studied the Art of War by Sima Rangju and Sun Tzu. The contents of these military classics can be summed up as 'three categories' and 'four methods.'"

VOLUME I

136

Emperor Taizong asked: "What are the 'three categories'?"

137

Li Jing replied: "I think the first category is the eighty-one articles in Taigong's Tactics on political and diplomatic conspiracies.

138

The second category is the seventy-one articles in Taigong's Speeches.

139

And the third category is the eighty-five articles in Taigong's Art of War.

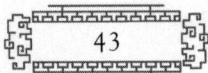

140

These teachings are profound. These are the 'three categories'."

141

Emperor Taizong asked: "What are the 'four methods'?"

142

Li Jing replied: "This was addressed by Ren Hong during the reign of Emperor Cheng of the Han Dynasty. He proposed four schools of warfare: military power and strategy, military situation, military yin and yang, and military skills. These are the 'four methods'."

143

Emperor Taizong asked: "The Methods of the Sima started by describing hunting in spring and winter. Why is that?"

144

Li Jing replied: "Hunting was held in the agricultural season to keep the troops in practice and to sacrifice to the temple to the gods.

145

This is to stress the importance of military governance.

146

In order to solemnise the matter, the kings of Zhou listed hunting as the most important system.

147

King Cheng of Zhou had hunting in the south of Mount Qishan; King Kang of Zhou received the courtesy of the lords in Feng Palace during the time of hunting, and King Mu of Zhou had hunting in Mount Tushan to meet the lords, all of which were personally hosted by the Son of Heaven.

148

After the decline of the Zhou Dynasty, Duke Huan of Qi met with the lords in Zhaoling and Duke Wen of Jin allied with the lords in Jiantu, both of which were done by the lords in the name of the Son of Heaven.

149

The purpose of hunting is to deter the lords who dare to disobey the king's orders.

150

In the name of the imperial meeting, the military training was conducted during hunting, which indicated that the state should not easily mobilise the army in peaceful time.

151

Agricultural season was used for hunting, which indicated that it is important not to forget the preparation for war.

152

That is why the Methods of the Sima put hunting first. Isn't it thought-provoking?"

153

Emperor Taizong asked: "According to the Zuo Zhuan, King Zhuang of Chu had two divisions of chariots: 'The hundred officers in the army act according to the call of the flag and drum, and the army is prepared without waiting for orders.' Was this also a system from the Zhou Dynasty?"

154

Li Jing replied: "According to the Zuo Zhuan, King Zhuang's two divisions of chariots had thirty vehicles in each division, and the number of soldiers in each vehicle was one hundred, which was twice as many as the number of soldiers per vehicle in the Zhou system.

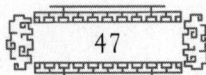

155

The foot-soldiers moved on the right side of the chariot, with the right handle of the chariot as the axis for combating and they fought between the chariots.

156

This was based on the system of the Zhou Dynasty.

157

I think that each chariot of Chu required one hundred and fifty foot-soldiers, which was more than the Zhou system.

158

In the Zhou system, there were seventy-two foot-soldiers and three armoured soldiers for each chariot.

159

So there were seventy-five in total, which was divided into three divisions with twenty-five men in each.

160

In the state of Chu, there were plenty of high mountains and large swamps.

161

Hence they had to use fewer chariots but more soldiers.

162

The system was the same as that of the Zhou dynasty, which also divided one hundred and fifty men into three divisions."

163

Emperor Taizong asked: "During the Spring and Autumn Period, Xun Wu of Jin led an army to invade Di, abandoning chariot warfare and replacing it with infantry warfare. Is it a use of regular forces or ad-hoc tactics?"

164

Li Jing replied: "Xun Wu was using the method of chariot warfare even though he gave up chariot and used infantry.

165

When entering the battle, he put one team in the left corner, one in the right corner, and the other in the front.

166

This division of three units was a chariot warfare method used for tens of thousands of chariots.

167

According to Cao Cao's Art of War: the attacking chariot had seventy-five men, divided into one unit in the front, one in the left corner and one in the right; the defending chariot had one unit, including ten cooks, five guards, five horses, and five men for cutting wood and carrying water, which were twenty-five men in total.

168

The total number of soldiers in the attacking and defending chariots was one hundred.

169

So in order to mobilise one hundred thousand men, you need thousands of chariots.

170

To be more specific, you need two thousand light and heavy chariots, which is an ancient method advocated by Xun Wu.

171

As for the the Han and Wei military systems, usually five chariots formed a team with a commander; ten chariots formed a division with a commander; one thousand chariots had one chief commander and an assistant one.

172

When the number of chariots increased, the same method was followed. My method derives from the ancient one: elite troops are composed of cavalry; combat troops are composed of half infantry and half cavalry; stationary troops are composed of infantry and chariots.

173

This method was strictly adhered to when I crossed dangerous terrain for thousands of lis to crush the Turks in the west. The ancient method of warfare is strict and neat; it should be valued by us."

174

Emperor Taizong returned from his visit to Lingzhou and summoned Li Jing and gave him a seat.

175

He asked Li: "I ordered Daozong and Ashina She'er to lead an army to conquer the Xueyantuo tribes, whose Tiele people were willing to submit and asked for Han Chinese officials, and I had already granted their request.

176

Xueyantuo tribe fled to the west. I was concerned that it would be a potential threat in the future, so I sent Li Ji to lead an army to crush it again. Now the northern desert areas have been pacified, but the local tribes are mixed with the the Han Chinese and barbarians. What method do you think can make the two sides live in peace for a long time?"

177

Li Jing replied: "Your Majesty has ordered to set up sixty-six post stations among the tribes from the Turkic region to Uyghur Khaganate to facilitate the transmission of information by scouts, which has been well planned.

178

However, I think that when it comes to training, Han soldiers should use the methods of Han, and barbarian soldiers should use the methods of barbarians; do not mix them up.

179

In the event of enemy invasion, the general shall be instructed to make the Han and barbarian troops temporarily exchange their banners and clothing, so that they can fight the enemy unexpectedly."

180

Emperor Taizong asked: "Why is that?"

181

Li Jing replied: "This approach is called 'taking various measures to cause confusion'.

182

If the barbarian soldiers pretend to be Han and the Han soldiers pretend to be barbarian, the enemy will not be able to tell the difference.

183

Then it will be impossible for them to find out our attack and defence plan.

184

He who is good at military governance shall 'mislead the enemy' by first making it impossible for them to figure out his intentions."

185

Emperor Taizong said: "What you said is exactly what I want; you can use this method to train the border generals.

186

By exchanging the banners and clothing of Han and barbarian soldiers, you show the art of regular and ad-hoc tactics."

187

Li Jing replied: "Your Majesty's wisdom is infinite and you infer other tactics from one fact.

188

I am so humbled that you praised my approach!"

189

Emperor Taizong asked: "Zhuge Liang once noted that 'A well-trained army with strict military discipline cannot be defeated even if the general is incompetent; an army lacking training and with lax military discipline cannot win a battle even if the general is very talented.' I do not think his statement is correct. What do you think?"

190

Li Jing replied: "He said it from experience.

191

According to Sun Tzu's Art of War: 'Chaos occurs when training and education are carried out without rules and regulations; when tense relations take place between officers and soldiers; and when disorganised and disordered military formations arise.' Since ancient times, there have been countless cases of self-inflicted destruction due to internal chaos in the army.

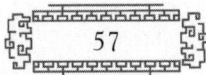

192

Mismanagement of military refers to the fact that the army training does not follow the ancient good practice; tense relationships between officers and soldiers refer to the fact that officers can not establish prestige; disordered formations refer to the fact that battle is lost not due to the strong enemy, but due to internal chaos.

193

Therefore Zhuge Liang also stated that 'When the army is well-trained and disciplined, although a mediocre general can win; otherwise, even a wise general cannot prevent dangers.' What is there to doubt about this?"

194

Emperor Taizong said: "Training and education are not to be neglected."

195

Li Jing said: "If training is done properly, the soldiers will gladly obey the orders.

196

If it is not done properly, even if you keep urging and scolding the soldiers from morning to evening, it will certainly not help! The reason why I have concentrated on writing the formations and systems of the ancients' military training into formation diagrams one by one is that I hope to train the troops into a master of discipline through these formations."

197

Emperor Taizong said: "Then I would like to see your diagrams of ancient formations."

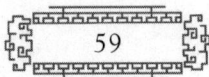

198

Emperor Taizong asked: "Barbarian soldiers often use charging horses to attack. Is this a use of ad-hoc tactics? Han soldiers in combat often use strong bows and crossbows to attack. Is this a use of regular tactics?"

199

Li Jing replied: "A good commander always tries to create a favourable condition, and does not put all the responsibilities on his subordinates; so he is able to select talents to create a favourable condition." The selection of talents mentioned here is to allow soldiers on both sides to give full play to their strengths in battle.

200

The barbarian soldiers are good at riding and shooting, which are suitable for swift strike.

201

And the Han soldiers are good at strong bows and crossbows, which are suitable for steady combat, which is to go with the flow.

202

This approach gives full play to their respective strengths; but it has nothing to do with the use of regular or ad-hoc tactics.

203

As I mentioned earlier, the soldiers from both Han and barbarians shall exchange their banners and costumes, and that is the interaction of regular and ad-hoc tactics.

204

Riding and shooting also imply regular tactics while bows and crossbows imply ad-hoc tactics. How can they be inflexible?"

205

Emperor Taizong said: "Please elaborate."

206

Li Jing replied: "This is the way to first deceive and lure the enemy and then put them under our control."

207

Emperor Taizong asked: "Recently the two tribes of Khitan and Xi have come to submit, I have set up two military offices in Songmo and Raole under the purview of Anbei government. I would like to appoint Xue Wanche as the governor. What do you think?"

208

Li Jing replied: "Xue is not as qualified as Ashina She'er, Zhishi Sili and Qibi Heli; these three barbarian officials are masters of military.

209

I have talked with them about the mountain and road conditions as well as the obedience and rebellion of barbarian tribes in Songmo and Raole.

210

We also discussed about a dozon of tribes in the western region.

211

Their remarks were clear and credible.

212

I taught them military formations and all showed admiration.

213

I hope that Your Majesty will appoint them without hesitation.

214

Xue is a man of courage but not strategy; he is not eligible for this position."

215

Emperor Taizong said: "You can use barbarians to serve for you! Our ancestors used to say: 'It is a permanent policy for China to control barbarians with barbarians.' You have definitely mastered this policy."

CHAPTER II.

VOLUME II

1

Emperor Taizong asked: "Among the various military books I have read, there is no one that can compare with Sun Tzu's Art of War; its thirteen chapters do not go beyond the discussion on weaknesses and strength.

2

If you can master the use of weaknesses and strength, you will be invincible.

3

Nowadays, generals talk too much about avoiding the enemy's strength and attacking their weaknesses.

4

But they fail to practice what they preach when they go to war because they cannot keep the enemy under control but are controlled by the enemy instead.

5

What do you think? Please elaborate on this for the generals to understand the essence of weaknesses and strength."

6

Li Jing replied: "It is necessary to first teach them the interactions of regular and ad-hoc tactics, and then the situation of perceiving weaknesses and strength.

7

Now most of the generals do not even know the interplay between regular and ad-hoc tactics.

8

How could they possibly understand the ideas of weaknesses and strength?"

9

Emperor Taizong asked: "You will know the enemy's gains and losses by analysing their situation; you will know the pattern of enemy movement by agitating them; you will know whether the enemy's terrain is favourable or not by various means of reconnaissance; you will know the enemy's advantages and disadvantages by attacking them. Is this the right way to use regular and ad-hoc tactics to find out the enemy's weaknesses and strength?"

10

Li Jing replied: "The use of regular and ad-hoc tactics is exactly about dealing with the enemy's weaknesses and strength. If the enemy are strong, I will use the regular forces; if the enemy are weak, I will use the ad-hoc forces. Without mastering the regular and ad-hoc tactics, a general will never win even when he finds out the weaknesses and strength of the enemy! So if I am ordered to teach the generals, they will first learn regular and ad-hoc tactics, and then they will naturally master the way to detect the weaknesses and strength of the enemy."

11

Emperor Taizong said: "When I change my ad-hoc forces into regular forces to strike, the enemy still think they are ad-hoc soldiers; when I change my regular forces into ad-hoc forces to attack, the enemy still think they are regular forces. In so doing, I can put the enemy in an unfavourable condition and myself in a favourable one. You should teach this method to the generals, so that they will see why they should learn it."

12

Li Jing replied: "To sum up from the teachings in thousands of chapters and sentences: 'to control the enemy and not to be controlled by the enemy'. I will teach this principle to the generals."

13

Emperor Taizong asked: "I set up a military office in Yaochi under the purview of Anxi government. What should I do with the Han and barbarian soldiers from that place?"

14

Li Jing replied: "All men are created equal without distinction between Han and barbarian.

15

But for those who are located in a remote desert area, they must live by shooting and hunting, so they fight that way.

16

If we comfort them with kindness and faith and give them relief in food and clothing, they will all be converted to Han Chinese.

17

Your Majesty has set up this office, and I request that the Han soldiers be taken back and placed in the interior region so as to reduce the transportation of food and materials.

18

This approach is what military strategists call the method of governing by strength.

19

Then select Han officials who are familiar with the situation of barbarians to guard their various fortresses.

20

This method will be sustainable. Once there is a critical situation, the Han soldiers will go out to fight."

21

Emperor Taizong asked: "What did Sun Tzu say about governing by strength is his Art of War?"

22

Li Jing replied: "He made a general statement that 'To be near the goal while the enemy is still far from it; to wait at ease while the enemy is toiling and struggling; to be well-fed while the enemy is famished'.

23

Those who are good at military governance will further develop these three points to six aspects: to wait for their arrival by luring the enemy to march forward; to wait for the enemy to be in disorder with calmness; to wait for the enemy's light troops with heavy troops; to wait for the enemy's slackness with seriousness; to wait for the enemy's confusion with rigour; and to wait for the enemy's attack with high alert.

24

Otherwise, we will lose. How can we command the army without governing its strength well?"

25

Emperor Taizong said: "Nowadays people study Sun Tzu's Art of War with plenty of preaching but without promoting its essence." This approach of governing by strength shall be learned by all the commanders."

26

Emperor Taizong asked: "There are not many veterans left with combat experience, and the existing army is newly formed and has not been in combat. What should be the best approach to training?"

27

Li Jing replied: "I used to train the army in three stages.

28

In the first stage, train soldiers in a unit of five before commanders take over.

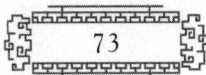

29

In the second stage, commanders trained soldiers in ten units of five and one hundred units of five.

30

In the third stage, the assistant general took over by training formations among all units of men.

31

The supreme general would then review the army after the three stages of training were completed; he would check the various formations, distinguish between regular and ad-hoc forces, admonish the commanders to give punishment for violation, and then the king would have a final review and send orders."

32

Emperor Taizong asked: "There have been several methods to form a unit of five. Which methods are the major ones?"

33

Li Jing replied: "According to the Zuo Zhuan, twenty-five chariots were a unit and five men were a unit; according to the Methods of the Sima, five men formed a unit; according to Wei Liao Zi, five men were in a unit for command; in the Han Dynasty, a system was founded to record military documents in bamboo slips and implement mutual management of soldiers in a unit of five.

34

This Han system was gradually abandoned as the later generation began to replace bamboo with paper.

35

I study all of these methods and conclude that units of five turned into units of twenty-five and then seventy-five; that is why in the Spring and Autumn Period, there were seventy-two foot-soldiers serving with three armoured soldiers.

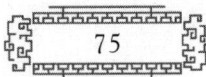

36

If there were no chariots, then twenty-five foot-soldiers and eight horses were used; this is also part of the system where a unit of five soldiers used five different weapons.

37

Therefore the idea of the units of five can be seen in various schools of thought.

38

In marching formations, there were five soldiers to form a short row and twenty-five to form a long row.

39

Then three long rows would be seventy-five men; fifteen long rows would be three hundred and seventy-five men.

40

Among them, three hundred men would be regular forces and sixty would be ad-hoc forces.

41

Then the regular and ad-hoc forces would be divided into two parts respectively.

42

In so doing, a marching formation would have an even number of soldiers on the left and right sides.

43

According to Sima Rangju, five men formed a unit and ten units of five formed a group. I follow his method, which is a principle of governing the units of five."

44

Emperor Taizong asked: "I have discussed the art of war with Li Ji; his insights are mostly the same as yours.

45

But he did not look into the original source.

46

You created the Hexagon Flower formation.

47

What is it based on?"

48

Li Jing replied: "It is based on Zhuge Liang's eightfold formation.

49

The basic principle is that the big formation contains the small formation; the big camp contains the small camp; the four corners of the four directions are connected to each other; and every movement corresponds to each other.

50

Zhuge Liang's eightfold formation followed these principles, so does my formation.

51

Therefore, the outside of my formation is shown in a square, and the inside of the central army is shown in a circle.

52

Its overall shape is like a hexagon-shaped flower; this is where the name comes from."

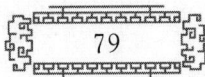

53

Emperor Taizong asked: "The inner formation is a circle and the outer formation is a square. What is this for?"

54

Li Jing replied: "The outside sixfold formation is square for regular forces; the inner central formation is round for ad-hoc forces.

55

The square is used to define the range of the battlefield, and the circle is used to connect the routes of manoeuvring.

56

Therefore, the number of steps to define the range of the battlefield should be as fixed as the earth; the route to determine the manoeuvring should be as flexible as the movement of the stars.

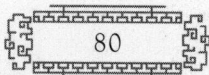

57

With a fixed number of steps and a neat gyration, it is possible to change in a way that is not prone to confusion.

58

The evolution from the eightfold formation to my Hexagon Flower formation has its origin in Zhuge Liang's principle."

59

Emperor Taizong said: "The outer square is to show the number of steps the soldiers take to advance and retreat, and the inner circle is to show the range of weapon use.

60

If you want to teach the steps to be accurate and the weapons to be flexible, you should teach the techniques so that the soldiers can well balance their hands and feet movements.

61

In so doing, the ancient methods are fulfilled!"

62

Li Jing replied: "Wu Zi said: 'The formations are divided but not separated; even when the troops retreat the ranks do not scatter.' This is the way to train steps.

63

Educating soldiers is like arranging pieces on a chessboard; if you don't draw a good route, where do the pieces move to?

64

As Sun Tzu put it, 'Measurement owes its existence to earth; estimation of quantity to measurement; calculation to estimation of quantity; balancing of chances to calculation; and victory to balancing of chances.

65

A victorious army against a routed one is as a pound's weight placed in the scale against a single grain.' The key is to estimate and measure the size and distance of terrain."

66

Emperor Taizong said: "What a remarkable observation of Sun Tzu!" How can we make the army move forward in rhythm without considering the distance and size of the terrain?"

67

Li Jing replied: "Mediocre generals have no idea what rhythm is all about.

68

'Therefore the good fighter will be furious in his onset and prompt in his decision.

69

His energy may be likened to the bending of a crossbow;
decision, to the releasing of a trigger.' I have studied this
approach: when it comes to the deployment of the army, it is
appropriate for soldiers to have an interval of ten steps; the
stationing troops are twenty steps away from the front troops.

70

A combat unit is set every two units of men.

71

Each move forward is fifty steps.

72

When the first horn is blown, each unit of soldiers at the same
time stands in a scattered formation; the interval does not
exceed ten steps.

73

Until the fourth horn, each unit kneels on the ground while holding spears.

74

Then hit the drum to send signals; each unit shouts three times and strikes three times, advancing to thirty to fifty steps away from the enemy to deal with changes of enemy formations.

75

Soldiers on horses then move forward from the rear and also advance to thirty to fifty steps away from the enemy.

76

The regular forces are followed by ad-hoc forces to observe the next moves by the enemy.

77

Then hit the drum again and send ad-hoc forces ahead of regular forces to lure the enemy.

78

Seize this opportunity to strike the enemy's weaknesses.

79

This is the basic principles of my Hexagon Flower formation."

80

Emperor Taizong asked: "According to the Art of War by Cao Cao: 'To set up a formation against the enemy, one must first set up a standard pillar, and then lead the army to set up a formation according to the position of the pillar. If a part of the army is attacked by the enemy, the rest who do not go to the rescue shall be beheaded.' What kind of strategy is this?"

81

Li Jing replied: "It is not correct to say that the pillar is set up only when facing the enemy; this is a training method instead.

82

The ancient strategists only taught regular tactics instead of ad-hoc tactics, and commanded the army like driving a flock of sheep, telling it to advance and retreat; the army ended up feeling lost about where to go.

83

Cao Cao was arrogant and ambitious; his commanders followed his Art of War and did not dare to point out his shortcomings.

84

If you set up a pillar only when the enemy is approaching as Cao proposed, isn't it too late? I see Your Majesty's 'Dance and Music for Disrupting Formation', where there are four banners in front and eight long streamers behind.

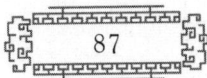

QUESTIONS AND REPLIES

85

Dancers either move to the left or to the right, spinning and turning in fast and slow steps.

86

Gongs and drums are beaten in their own rhythm.

87

This is the way to imitate the four parts in front and eight parts behind of the eightfold formation.

88

Ordinary people only appreciate the tremendous performance of music and dance, but they do not know about its demonstration of military formation!"

89

Emperor Taizong said: "After the Emepror Gaozu of Han had conquered the world, he wrote the Song of the Great Wind; one of the lines is: 'Where will I find brave men to guard the four corners of my land?' The art of war can be understood, but not expressed in words.

90

You are the only one who knows the true meaning of my 'Dance and Music for Disrupting Formation'.

91

The future generations will see that I did not just create it for entertainment."

92

Emperor Taizong asked: "There is a practice of directing the movement of the army with flags of five colours in five directions.

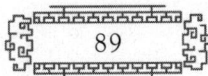

93

Is this for the regular tactics? As for directing the army with long streamers and small flags, is this for the ad-hoc tactics? How can the number of army units be appropriate when they are divided and changed?"

94

Li Jing replied: "I refer to the ancient method: if five units are combined into one, then two flags are crossed; and if ten units are combined into one, then five flags are crossed.

95

When dispersed, blow a horn and separate the crossed five flags, then the one unit is divided into ten; for the unit with two flags crossed, it will be divided into five; for the unit with two flags that are not crossed, it will be divided into three.

96

When the formation is scattered, change it to a concentrated one as an ad-hoc strategy; when it is assembled, change it to a scattered one as an ad-hoc strategy.

97

After implementing three orders and five decrees and three times of dividing formations and using ad-hoc tactics, it is time to go back to the drill of the regular forces for the eightfold formation with four parts in front and eight behind.

98

These are the steps of training formations."

99

Emperor Taizong commended Li Jing.

100

Emperor Taizong asked: "Cao Cao deployed vanguard cavalry, combat cavalry and reconnaissance cavalry. What about today's deployment of cavalry?"

101

Li Jing replied: "Cao's Art of War stated that vanguard cavalry was deployed in the front, combat cavalry in the middle and reconnaissance cavalry in the back.

102

He named the three units according to their different tasks.

103

According to the ancient system, eight units of cavalry have twenty-four chariot soldiers and twenty-four units of cavalry have seventy-two chariot soldiers.

104

Regular tactics are for chariot soldiers while ad-hoc tactics are for horse-riding soldiers.

105

Cao divided cavalry into three parts without any deployment on the left and right sides.

106

This is just one strategy.

107

People do not get this strategy and wrongly presume that vanguard cavalry must be in front of the combat and reconnaissance cavalry.

108

My method is that, as the formations change, reconnaissance cavalry goes first, followed by vanguard and combat cavalry.

109

This move was also adopted by Cao Cao."

110

Emperor Taigong said: "There are so many people who are confused by Cao Cao in this respect."

111

Emperor Taizong asked: "The principle of the use of chariot soldiers, infantry and cavalry is the same. So is it the role of men that matters?"

112

Li Jing replied: "A formation called 'Entrapping the Fish' was practised in the Spring and Autumn Period with chariots in the front followed by infantry.

113

At the time, there were only chariot soldiers and infantry with an absence of cavalry.

114

The formation was divided into two parts on the left and right sides to defend without using ad-hoc tactics.

115

When Xun Wu of Jin attacked Di, he abandoned chariots and used infantry and increased the number of cavalry to attack.

116

This is the use of ad-hoc tactics to strike instead of to defend.

117

I have drawn upon merits of them: use one horse-riding soldier to replace three foot-soldiers; adjust the numbers of chariot and foot-soldiers.

118

I combine the units of chariot soldiers, infantry and cavalry; then how would the enemy know about my attack routes by these three units of soldiers? Military deployment shall be as secretive as things moving underground or as unavoidable as things falling from sky.

119

Such a mastery of war is Your Majesty's genius that I can never reach."

120

Emperor Taizong asked: "Taigong stated that: 'Draw the place where the formation is laid out as a square; each side is six hundred steps or sixty steps long; then mark out in the order of the twelve hours' What do you think of this method?"

121

Li Jing replied: "Draw a square for the formation with a perimeter of one thousand and two hundred steps.

122

Each small part occupies a small square of twenty steps on all sides with one person for every five steps in the horizontal direction and one person for every four steps in the vertical direction.

123

Then a total of two thousand and five hundred people form five big square formations in the east, west, south, north and central place.

124

The four corners are empty.

125

This is called formations within a formation.

126

When King Wu of the Zhou attacked the Shang army, his ministries deployed three thousand warriors in each unit.

127

Each formation had six thousand men; and they had thirty thousand men in five formations in total.

128

This is consistent with the principle of how Taigong drew the layout of formations."

129

Emperor Taizong asked: "How do you draw your layout of the Hexagon Flower Formation?"

130

Li Jing replied: "In the place of the army review, I draw a square with a perimeter of one thousand and two hundred steps; then I distinguish the big square into six formations, and each formation occupies a smaller square with a perimeter of four hundred steps.

131

Then I divide the six formations into two sections in the east and west while leaving empty the square with a perimeter of one thousand and two hundred steps in the middle for training.

132

I train thirty thousand soldiers with five thousand in each formation.

133

One formation is to practice the method of stationing camp, while the other five formations are to practice the square, round, curved, straight and sharp changes of formation.

134

Each formation changes five times, and five formations change twenty-five times in total."

135

Emperor Taizong asked: "Why do you use five formations?"

136

Li Jing replied: "They are originally based on the name of the five colours representing five directions.

137

The square, round, curved, straight and sharp formations are based on different terrain.

138

If the army is not familiar with these five formations, how can they fight against the enemy? All warfare is based on deception.

139

Therefore, the formations are deliberately divided into five.

140

The purpose is to conceal their deceitfulness and illustrate the truth that they are both inclusive and exclusive.

QUESTIONS AND REPLIES

141

In fact, the movement of the army is like water; the direction of its flow is restricted by the terrain of war. This is the true meaning of five formations."

142

Emperor Taizong asked: "Li Ji mentioned the methods called Pin Mu, Square and Circle and Ambush. Did ancient strategists use them?"

143

Li Jing replied: "The method of Pin Mu derived from legend.

144

It simply means yin and yang.

145

Fan Li once observed: 'To use potential for a later attack, and to use sharpness for a first attack; to fold the enemy's sharpness to the minimum, and to use our potential to the maximum to destroy the enemy.' This is the true meaning of mastering yin and yang in warfare.

146

Fan Li also noted that: 'Lay out the right formation as the yin and the left formation as the yang; the early and late combat should be in accordance with the time of the day.' That is to say, the right and left of the formation and the early and late action shall be planned according to the situation, which lies in the change of regular and ad-hoc tactics.

147

Left and right refer to the yin and yang; right is yin and left is yang.

148

Morning and evening refer to the yin and yang of the sky; evening is yin and morning is yang.

149

The use of regular and ad-hoc tactics refers to the interactions of left and right and morning and evening.

150

Without any changes, the difference between yin and yang would be meaningless.

151

So what deceives the enemy is to confuse it with ad-hoc forces, not our regular forces; and what defeats the enemy is to strike it with regular forces, not our ad-hoc forces.

152

This is the interaction of regular and ad-hoc tactics.

153

The real ambush is not only the use of soldiers hiding and waiting among grass and trees to set up an ambush.

154

Instead, ambush is about using regular forces as steadily and firmly as a mountain and using ad-hoc forces as sharply and swiftly as a thunder.

155

In so doing, the enemy can never tell our regular and ad-hoc tactics. Then the use of tactics will leave no clue for the enemy to find."

156

Emperor Taizong asked: "What is the rationale for the formations of the four beasts: dragon, tiger, bird and snake, and the four scale of Re, Mi, So and Fa to represent them?"

157

Li Jing replied: "This is the warfare deception."

158

Emperor Taizong asked: "Can it be abolished?"

159

Li Jing replied: "To preserve them is precisely for the purpose of abolishing them. If they are to abolished, more methods of deceptions will arise."

160

Emperor Taizong asked: "Why is that?"

161

Li Jing replied: "Borrowing the names of the four beasts of the dragon, tiger, bird and snake or the titles of heaven, earth, wind and cloud, together with the scales of Re, Mi, Fa, So and elements of metal, water, fire and wood is traditionally used for warfare deception. If these names are retained, then other deceitful methods will not be added; otherwise, the greedy and foolish people will resort to other means."

162

Emperor Taizong contemplated for a long time before saying: "You have to keep it a secret and not to divulge it."

163

Emperor Taizong said: "I am suspicious of the statement that one shall make the three armies afraid of the monarch but not the enemy by using severe punishment and harsh laws.

164

Emperor Guangwu of Han resisted Wang Mang's millions of troops with a lone army and did not use severe punishment and harsh laws. Why is that?"

165

Li Jing replied: "The conditions of victory and defeat vary widely and differently, and cannot be inferred from one condition.

166

Chen Sheng and Wu Guang defeated the Qin army, but can we say that their criminal law was harsher than Qin?

167

The reason why Emperor Guangwu waged war was because he responded to the people's resentment against Wang Mang, not to mention that Wang Mang's commanders Wang Xun and Wang Yi did not know the art of war.

168

That is why they were defeated despite their large number of troops.

169

According to Sun Tzu's Art of War: 'If soldiers are punished before they have grown attached to you, they will not prove submissive; if they are submissive and attached to you but not subject to punishment, then they will be practically useless.' Therefore a general must first bond with his soldiers with kindness and love.

170

If he does not have a good relationship with his men, he cannot succeed by resorting to stringent punishment."

171

Emperor Taizong asked: "But the Book of Documents made different remarks: 'If majesty exceeds benevolence, you can succeed; if benevolence exceeds strictness, you will not succeed.' What does this mean then?"

172

Li Jing replied: "Benevolence and love shall come first before punishment. The order shall not be reversed.

173

If you use punishment first and then benevolence to remedy the situation, it will not help.

174

The Book of Documents emphasised authority over love to admonish people to carefully consider the authority of the decrees after committing offences; it is not an approach for education before offences.

175

Therefore, Sun Tzu's principle shall be universal for all generations to follow."

176

Emperor Taizong asked: "After you defeated Xiao Xi's army, all the commanders tended to confiscate the family fortune of the civil and military officials under Xiao to reward soldiers.

177

You disapproved of that and cited the incident of Emperor Gaozu deciding not to kill Kuai Tong before the people of Jianghan submitted to Gaozu.

178

It reminds me of an ancient saying: 'Civil virtues convince the soldiers, and martial virtues deter the enemy.' That is what you believe in, isn't it?"

179

Li Jing replied: "After Emperor Guangwu of Han contained the Chimei army, he entered the Chimei camp on horseback slowly and inspected the camp to show that he had no suspicion of Chimei.

180

The Chimei army said to him: 'Your Majesty has come here with sincerity.

181

Because you have already known that the Chimei army are good people.

182

Otherwise you would not have entered our camp without caution!' When I was conquering the Turks, I led both Han and barbarian soldiers for thousands of lis out of the fortress without killing anyone during the process.

183

I treated my men with sincerity and selflessness.

184

Your Majesty trusted me so much and had promoted me to this senior position.

185

I am tremendously humbled to claim that I have both civil and martial virtues."

186

Emperor Taizong asked: "I once sent Tang Jian as an envoy to the Turkic region, but you took advantage of this opportunity by attacking them. Some say that you were using Tang Jian as a death spy. I still have doubts about it. What do you think?"

187

Li Jing bowed and replied: "Tang Jian and I both assisted the monarch; I did not expect Tang Jian to be able to convince the Turks.

188

Therefore, I attacked when the Turks let down their guard. This is to get rid of the threat to our state, so I could not care less about my personal relationship with Tang Jian. Some say that I took Tang Jian as a death spy, which is not my intention.

189

Sun Tzu's Art of War stated that using spies is the last resort.

190

'Water can carry a boat as well as overturn it.' So there are those who succeed in using spies, and those who fail.

191

If a minister assists the ruler from a young age, participates in the imperial government with impartiality and loyalty, and does not deceive and meets with sincerity, then how come the use of spies affects his reputation? The example of Tang Jian is just a minor issue. Why should Your Majesty doubt it?"

192

Emperor Taizong said: "Indeed, it is not true that people who are benevolent and righteous cannot use spies; a mediocre man is incapable of using spies. The Duke of Zhou also killed his relatives for the sake of great righteousness, not to mention somebody as an envoy. Now I understand without a doubt."

193

Emperor Taizong asked: "In warfare, let your great objective be fighting in your own state, not in a foreign state and fighting in a swift manner not in a protracted manner. Why is that?"

194

Li Jing replied: "Warfare is only a last resort, so it is not advisable to fight in a foreign state and for a long time. As Sun Tzu's Art of War put it, 'Contributing to maintain an army at a distance causes the people to be impoverished'.

195

This is the disadvantage of fighting in a foreign state.

196

Sun Tzu also argued that 'The skilful soldiers do not raise a second levy, neither are their supply-wagons loaded three times.' This is the lessons learned for fighting in a protracted war.

VOLUME II

197

I have studied the situations of fighting in one's own state and in foreign states and concluded a method to convert one to the other."

198

Emperor Taizong asked: "What is that?"

199

Li Jing replied: "'To take food from the enemy' is to change a foreign war to a domestic one.

200

'If the enemy is at ease, wear them down; if they are well supplied with food, starve them out.' This is to change a domestic war of the enemy to a foreign one.

201

Therefore, it is not necessary to stick to the ideas of foreign, domestic, swift and protracted war. As long as we can command properly, we will win."

202

Emperor Taizong asked: "Is there such an example in the past?"

203

Li Jing replied: "When Yue invaded Wu, they used the left and right armies to beat the drums to enter the battle, and the Wu army divided to resist.

204

Then the central army of Yue stopped drum-beating and crossed rivers to ambush Wu.

205

This is an example of turning a foreign war into a domestic one.

206

When Shi Le fought against Ji Tan, Ji Tan led his troops from afar and Shi Le sent Kong Chang as the vanguard to meet Ji Tan's army.

207

Kong deliberately retreated to lure Ji's army to chase him, while Shi Le used ambush troops in a pincer attack and defeated Ji's army.

208

This is an example or turning hard toil into ease. Examples like these from the past abound."

209

Emperor Taizong asked: "Iron caltrops and chevaux de frise were invented by Taigong, correct?"

210

Li Jing replied: "Yes, but they were only used to defend against the enemy.

211

The important thing is to defeat the enemy, not just to stop them.

212

The iron caltrops and chevaux de frise mentioned in Taigong's Six Secret Teachings were tools for defence, not for attack."

CHAPTER III.

VOLUME III

1

Emperor Taizong asked: "Taigong argued that 'When fighting with infantry against chariots and cavalry, one must rely on hillocks, ravines, and treacherous and obstructed terrain.' However, Sun Tzu claimed that 'Armies must not stop in the land with crevasses, hillocks, ravines, and the ruins of uninhabited cities and towns.' What do you think?

2

Li Jing replied: "To fight with an army is to unify the will, and to unify the will is to prohibit rumours and eliminate suspicions.

3

If the general has doubts, then the army will be shaken.

4

And if the army is shaken, then the enemy will take advantage of the opportunity to attack.

5

Camping is used to facilitate the manoeuvring of the army.

6

Where there are precipitous cliffs with torrents running between, deep natural hollows, quagmires and crevasses, the army shall leave immediately to prevent the enemy to take advantage of the opportunity to attack.

7

As for hillocks, ravines, and the ruins of uninhabited cities and towns, how can we fight without making use of them? Taigong's statement is the most important principle of using the army."

8

Emperor Taizong asked: "I think there is nothing more violent than war in the world.

9

In warfare, how can we hesitate about things that are conducive to the fight?

10

If our commanders fail to seize the opportunity because they are stuck with the yin and yang divination, you should warn them against it."

11

Li Jing bowed and replied: "According to Wei Liao Zi: 'The Yellow Emperor used benevolence and virtue to settle the world, and used force to crush the enemy.'

12

This is what strategists say about punishment and virtue, which are way superior to the theories on celestial phenomena concerning times and dates.

13

However, it is important to let people use deception without letting them know why.

14

Mediocre and incompetent generals often stick to yin and yang divination and thus fail to win; we must learn the lessons.

15

I will immediately declare to the commanders Your Majesty's admonition."

16

Emperor Taizong asked: "The use of military force can be scattered or concentrated, and each must be used in its own way. Who was skilled at this in the past?"

17

Li Jing replied: "In the Qin Dynasty, Fu Jian led an army of one million and was defeated in Fei Shui, which was the result of using the army together but not separately.

18

When Wu Han attacked Gongsun Shu, Wu and his assistant commander Liu Shang camped thirty *li* away and then joined to defeat Gongsun Shu.

19

This was the result of mobilising separated troops to fight together.

20

Taigong noted that: 'When it is time to separate and the army fails to do it, the army is restrained; when it is time to fight together and the army fails to do it, it is isolated'."

21

Emperor Taizong said: "Fu Jian initially conquered the Central Plains region because he appointed Wang Meng, who knew the art of war well; and after Wang Meng's death, Fu Jian was defeated in Fei Shui due to his restrained troops! On the other hand, Wu Han was trusted by Emperor Guangwu of Han and he was not restrained by the imperial court, so Wu was able to conquer Shu thanks to the fact that his army was not isolated! The successes and failures of the previous generations can serve as a reference for future generations."

22

Emperor Taizong asked: "I have read lots of military classics of thousands of chapters and sentences, but the principle or warfare can be summed up as 'to use multiple methods to make the enemy make mistakes'."

23

Li Jing contemplated for long and replied: "Your Majesty is right.

24

In warfare, if the enemy do not make mistakes, then how can our army achieve victory?

25

It is similar to a close game of chess.

26

A wrong move can make you lose everything.

27

Most of the victories and defeats are due to one single mistake, not to mention multiple mistakes."

28

Emperor Taizong asked: "Attack and defence are two means to the same end.

29

As Sun Tzu's Art of War put it, 'When a general is skilful in attack, his opponent does not know what to defend; and when he is skilful in defence, his opponent does not know what to attack.' But he did not speak of the situation in which I strike back when the enemy come to attack me and I defend when the enemy also carry out defence.

30

What method should be used to win when both sides are attacking and defending at the same time?"

31

Li Jing replied: "There were many cases of attacking and defending each other at the same time.

32

It was said that 'defending is a lack of strength, and attacking is a surplus of strength.' Some thought that a lack of strength inevitably implied weaknesses and a surplus of strength, power.

33

They did not master the art of managing attack and defence.

34

According to Sun Tzu's Art of War, 'Defend when you cannot win and attack when you can.' That is to say, when it is unlikely to defeat the enemy, one shall temporarily defend; when the conditions for victory are created, one shall attack.

35

This approach is not necessarily about one's strength or weakness.

36

People who did not understand it decided to defend when they were supposed to attack and attack when they were supposed to defend; they violated the principle of both attack and defence, so they could not adopt a unified strategy of the two."

37

Emperor Taizong said: "You are right.

38

The surplus or deficiency of forces made them doubt the strength of the force.

39

They did not know that the principle of defence is to pretend to the enemy that there is a lack of strength, and the principle of attack is to pretend to the enemy that there is sufficient strength.

40

If we pretend to have insufficient strength, the enemy are bound to attack, and this is to make the enemy unaware of their improper timing of attack.

41

If we pretend to have excessive strength, the enemy will inevitably turn to defence, which is to make them unaware of their wrong timing of defence.

42

Attack and defence are both used as one unified strategy to win; but from the perspective of the enemy and us, the two shall also be discussed separately.

43

If I do it properly, the enemy will fail; if the enemy do it properly, I will fail.

44

Results tell who is the master of the strategy.

45

Attack and defence are one unified strategy to win, and if we master this strategy, we will win a hundred battles.

46

That is why Sun Tzu concluded that: 'If you know the enemy and know yourself, you need not fear the result of a hundred battles.' This is the purpose of mastering attack and defence."

47

Li Jing bowed and replied: "What a profound strategy! Attack is the transformation of defence, and defence is the means of attack; both are used to defeat the enemy.

48

If one attacks without preparing for defence and defends without preparing for attacks, then he treats attack and defence as two separate matters, and sets apart the use of attack and defence.

49

Then even though one can recite the Art of War by Sun Tzu and Wu Zi, if he cannot understand the subtleties of its application and takes attack and defence as two opposing strategies, then how can he know the true meaning of the art of war!"

50

Emperor Taizong asked: "According to the Methods of the Sima, 'Although a state is strong, if it is keen on war, it will surely perish; although the world is peaceful, if it neglects the danger of war, it will surely put itself in a perilous situation.' Is this also about attack and defence?"

51

Li Jing replied: "There are no states that do not stress the importance of attack and defence.

52

Attack is not only attacking the enemy's city and camp, but also the way to destroy their morale.

53

Defence is not only about solid fortresses and military formations, but also about keeping our morale high and seizing the opportunity to disrupt the enemy.

54

What I have said above is what a king should know as a general principle.

55

It is also a specific method that a general should master.

56

To demoralise the enemy is to know the enemy; to boost our moral is to know ourselves."

57

Emperor Taizong said: "You are right.

58

Whenever I face the enemy in battle, I first try to find out whose plan is more well-organised to see the strength and weaknesses of the two sides.

59

Then I try to find out whose morale is higher to see the strength and weaknesses of the two sides.

60

Therefore, knowing the enemy and oneself is a crucial principle in the art of war.

61

Nowadays, even when a general does not know the enemy's situation, if he can know his own situation, how can he still lose?"

62

Li Jing replied: "Sun Tzu noted that: 'The good fighters first put themselves beyond the possibility of defeat.' This is to know oneself; 'Then they waited for an opportunity of defeating the enemy.' This is to know the enemy.

63

He added: 'To secure ourselves against defeat lies in our own hands, but the opportunity of defeating the enemy is provided by the enemy himself by his mistakes.' I do not dare to violate this teaching at all when I command the army."

64

Emperor Taizong asked: "Sun Tzu's Art of War commented on how the enemy army can be robbed of their spirit: 'A soldier's spirit is keenest in the morning; by noonday it has begun to flag; and in the evening, his mind is bent only on returning to camp.

65

A clever general, therefore, avoids an army when its spirit is keen, but attacks it when it is sluggish and inclined to return.

66

This is the art of studying moods.' What do you think?"

67

Li Jing replied: "Anyone who is active and energetic can summon up the courage to fight the enemy and be fearless of death; this is the role of spirit.

68

So in order to mobilise our troops, we shall motivate their fighting spirit and inspire their courage to overcome the enemy, so that we can advance to attack the enemy.

69

Among the four key factors proposed by Wu Zi, morale came first.

70

If we can make everyone brave enough to fight on their own, their fierce power cannot be stopped.

71

As a matter of fact, the high spirit in the morning does not limit morale to a particular moment; it is only a metaphor.

72

If the enemy's morale does not recede after three attacks, how can one be sure that they will certainly be worn-out and fail? If he who learns the art of war only blindly sticks to written words, he will be tricked by the enemy.

73

But if he knows the principle of how to demoralise the enemy, he will be competent to command his troops in battle."

74

Emperor Taizong asked: "You have said that Li Ji knows the art of war, then can I entrust him with a long-serving position? I am afraid that if I do not rein in him, he would not serve the government for long. And how can my son manage him in the future?"

75

Li Jing replied: "For Your Majesty's sake, why don't you remove him from his post? In the future you son will appoint him again, then he will surely be grateful for the reward. No harm would be done this way."

76

Emperor Taizong said: "Excellent! Now I have no doubts about this."

77

Emperor Taizong asked: "If Li Ji and Zhangsun Wuji are in charge of the state affairs together, what will happen in the future?"

78

Li Jing replied: "Li is a loyal minister; I can guarantee that he is a competent official.

79

As for Zhangsun Wuji, he has made great contribution to assisting Your Majesty to govern the state, and Your Majesty has appointed him as an assistant minister.

80

Although he is modest and humble on the surface, he is cynical about the ability of the virtuous officials.

81

So Yuchi Jingde once accused him to his face, and then left (for fear of his revenge).

82

Hou Junji hated him for forgetting about their old friendship and thus participated in the rebellion led by the abolished prince Chengqian.

83

This was all caused by Zhangsun Wuji.

84

Since Your Majesty asked me about it, I dare not hold out on you."

85

Emperor Taizong said: "Do not divulge our discussions. I will think about it before making a decision."

86

Emperor Taizong said: "Emperor Gaozu of Han was good at commanding his generals, but later Han Xin and Peng Yue were killed and Xiao He was imprisoned. Why did he treat his meritorious officials this way?"

87

Li Jing replied: "I think either Liu Bang the Emperor Gaozu of Han or Xiang Yu the head of state of Chu was a competent commander.

88

When the state of Qin fell, Zhang Liang wanted to avenge the state of Han, and Chen Ping and Han Xin resented Xiang Yu for not assigning them senior positions, so they turned to Liu Bang to find a way out for themselves.

89

As for Xiao He, Cao Shen, Fan Kuai and Guan Ying, they were all outlaws who defected to Liu Bang, who conquered the world because he employed them.

90

If the descendants of the six states had been restored, they would have left Liu Bang because they missed their old kings, and even if Liu Bang had the talent as an imperial general, how could they decide to serve him? I think Liu Bang succeeded thanks to Zhang Liang's strategies and Xiao He's skills.

91

The killing of Han Xin and Peng Yue, and the non-appointment of Fan Zeng are due to the same reason.

92

That is why I said neither Liu Bang nor Xiang Yu was a competent commander."

93

Emperor Taizong asked: "After the reforms conducted by Emperor Guangwu of Han, he did not let meritorious officials be in charge of the imperial government in order to protect them. Is that correct?"

94

Li Jing replied: "Although Emperor Guangwu could easily succeed with the foundation of his predecessors, it is still remarkable for him to overthrow Wang Mang, whose power was no less than Xiang Yu, while his assistants Deng Yu and Kou Xun's talent was no match for Xiao He and Zhang Liang.

95

He managed to treat people with sincerity and use moderate policies to protect his meritorious officials, which was a wiser approach than Emperor Gaozu.

96

I think Guangwu was successful in the way he governed commanders."

97

Emperor Taizong asked: "In ancient times, when appointing a general for a battle, the king would first fast for three days, and then hand the general the battle-axe, saying: 'From now on, the general has full authority to handle all matters from this to heaven above.'

98

Then he would continue: 'From now on, the general has full authority to deal with all matters from this to the depths below.'

99

And he would push a chariot and said: 'The army will move in and out at the general's discretion according to the situation.' After the departure, the army would only listen to the general's command and not wait for the king's order.

100

I thought this ritual had been abandoned long ago.

101

Now I would like to work out with you the etiquette of dispatching the general with reference to the ancient rites. What do you think?"

102

Li Jing replied: "I think the rituals established by the sages in the ancestral temples are to grant the battle-axe and push the chariot in the name of god and grant the general military authority.

103

Now whenever Your Majesty go out to fight, you consult with the ministers first, and offer sacrifices to the ancestral temple before sending the general, so the ritual of assuming the authority of god is done; whenever you appoint the general, you advise him to act according to the opportunity, which means you grant them great authority.

104

What is the difference between your practice and the old practice of fasting and pushing chariot! Your approach is completely in line with the ancient rules, and bears the same meaning. So there is no need to change to the old rituals."

105

Emperor Taizong said: Excellent." He then ordered his ministers to record these two things as the law for the future dispatch of the general.

106

Emperor Taizong asked: "Can yin and yang divination be abolished?"

107

Li Jing replied: "No. Warfare is the art of deception. And the use of yin and yang divination is a way to use greedy and foolish people, so it cannot be abolished."

108

Emperor Taizong said: "But you have said that the celestial phenomena are not advocated by a wise general, only the incompetent general is restricted by them. Then it makes sense to abolish this practice."

109

Li Jing replied: "In the past, King Zhou of Shang was destroyed on the day of the Jia Zi (which began the cycle of sixty days in the traditional Stems-and-Branches in ancient China), while King Wu of Zhou was successful on another day of the Jia Zi.

110

According to theories on celestial phenomena, different results of the fall of Shang and the rise of Zhou both took place on the day of the Jia Zi.

111

Emperor Wu of Song decided to lead his army to invade Southern Yan on the "day of death", so his men tried to dissuade him.

112

He replied: 'It means it is the death of my enemy, not me.' He succeeded in conquering the enemy as a result.

113

Therefore it seems to be evident that the divination of yin and yang should be abolished.

114

However, when the Qi general Tian Dan was besieged by the Yan army, he ordered a man to pretend to be a master of divination and host sacrifice; the man said: 'The Yan army can be destroyed.' So Tian Dan attacked by means of charging bulls with their tails on fire and defeated the Yan army.

115

This is the way of military deception.

116

It shows how celestial phenomena can be used."

117

Emperor Taizong asked: "Tian Dan defeated the Yan army in the name of divination, but Taigong destroyed Shang by burning grass and tortoise used for divination. They used opposite approaches [but both succeeded]. Why is that?"

118

Li Jing replied: "Their motive of strengthening the army was the same; however, some people chose to take opposite approach and succeeded while some acted according to the situation at that time.

119

When Taigong assisted King Wu to conquer Shang, he marched to Muye and encountered thunder and downpour; his banners and drums were all destroyed.

120

The strategist San Yisheng wanted to ask for good fortune before taking action.

121

The army was hesitant and fearful at that time, so he had to ask the gods by divination to calm the army's mind.

122

Taigong, however, thought that there was no need to ask the gods by burning grass and tortoise.

123

They were trying to rebel against the king, so how could he afford to wait for an auspicious time before taking action? It seems that the motive of the divination to strengthen the army's morale was in the first place, and the motive of abandoning divination to strengthen the army's mind was in the second place.

124

But they did it for the same purpose despite their different approaches.

125

That is why I said earlier that the yin and yang divination should not be abolished in order to use this approach to prevent any possible problems.

126

But the key to success is the role of men."

127

Emperor Taizong asked: "The only commanders who are now in charge are Li Ji, Li Daozong, and Xue Wanche. Among these three, Daozong is a relative of mine. Who else shall I give an important position?"

128

Li Jing replied: "Your Majesty had said that Li Ji and Li Daozong would not win or lose a big battle, but Xue Wancher Fang would either win a great victory or have a great defeat.

129

I have been reflecting on Your Majesty's comments.

130

Not seeking a great victory nor having a great defeat means that the army acts with restraint; but having either a great victory or a great defeat means that the victory may be secured by luck.

131

That is why Sun Tzu argued that: 'The skilful fighter puts himself into a position which makes defeat impossible, and does not miss the moment for defeating the enemy.' The management of restraint lies in our decision."

132

Emperor Taizong asked: "How can it be done when we do not want to fight against each other as both sides meet?"

133

Li Jing replied: "When the Jin army fought against Qin, both sides retreated as soon as they came into contact.

134

As the Methods of the Sima put it: 'Do not chase a defeated enemy too far, and do not follow a retreating enemy too closely by managing your horses.' This remark implied that reins of the horses shall be managed to restrain the army.

135

When our army's movement is restrained and the enemy's ranks are solid, how can we fight easily? That is why two armies may decide to retreat without chasing to prevent defeat.

QUESTIONS AND REPLIES

136

Sun Tzu noted that: 'To refrain from intercepting an enemy whose banners are in perfect order; to refrain from attacking an army drawn up in calm and confident array – this is the art of studying circumstances.' It is natural that if both sides are evenly matched, when one side advances rashly, the enemy may take advantage and win.

137

Therefore, in warfare, some circumstances are for fighting, while some for not fighting.

138

Choosing not to fight is because we are not adequately prepared; choosing to fight is because we can take advantage to win."

139

Emperor Taizong asked: "What do you mean by not being adequately prepared?"

140

Li Jing replied: "Sun Tzu observed that: 'When I wish to avoid battle, I may defend myself simply be drawing a line on the ground; the enemy will be unable to attack me because I divert him from going where he wishes.' If the enemy has someone who is good at commanding, it is difficult to win when the two armies confront each other.

141

That is why I said choosing not to fight is because we are not adequately prepared.

142

We shall fight when we can take advantage of the enemy.

143

As Sun Tzu noted: 'Thus, he who is skilful in keeping the enemy on the move puzzle the enemy with deceptive appearances according to which the enemy will act.

144

He lures the enemy with a bait which they are certain to take.

145

He moves the enemy with small profit and ambush them.' Then if the enemy general is not competent, he will certainly come rashly for a fight, then we shall take advantage of the opportunity to defeat the enemy.

146

That is why I said that choosing to fight is because we can take advantage to win."

147

Emperor Taizong said: "The principle of restraint is profound! If you master this principle, you will win, and if you violate it, you will lose.

148

You can compile the examples of army governance from the past, and submit them in diagrams.

149

I would like to select the best of them to pass on to future generations."

150

Li Jing replied: "I previously submitted detailed formation diagrams of the Yellow Emperor, Taigong, the Methods of the Sima and Zhuge Liang's use of regular and ad-hoc forces.

151

Many of the famous generals of the past generations succeeded in adopting those principles But few ministers and officials knew how to govern the military, so they failed to record the actual events of war.

152

I will definitely comply with Your Majesty's order to compile and report to you."

153

Emperor Taizong asked: "Which is the most profound theory of art of war?"

154

Li Jing replied: "I have divided the art of war into three levels, so that those who study it can gradually progress and become proficient.

155

The first level is 'the Way'; the second level is heaven and earth; and the third level is command.

156

'The Way' is extremely sophisticated and subtle.

157

As I Ching concluded, the wisest man is able to make people submit without threatening to kill or torture.

158

Heaven refers to night and day; earth refers to danger and ease.

159

A wise general can use the night to win victories that are difficult to achieve during the day, and he can use unfavourable terrain to attack the enemy who occupy favourable terrain.

160

This is what Mencius meant by acquiring favourable timing, geographical and human conditions.

161

Command refers to the appointment of wise men and the use of good weapons.

162

This is what the Three Strategies meant by using wise and capable men to win and what Guan Zhong meant by only using sharp and solid weapons."

163

Emperor Taizong said: "Exactly.

164

I think that the one who makes the enemy surrender without fighting is superior; the one who wins a hundred battles is of a medium level; and the one who defends with deep ditches, high barriers and firm formations is inferior.

165

In this respect, Sun Tzu's Art of War is inclusive of all of these ideas."

166

Li Jing said: "Reading the articles and observing the deeds of the ancients help us to see their differences.

167

For example, Zhang Liang, Fan Li and Sun Tzu retired after their successes without a care in the world, if they had not known the subtleties of the 'Way', how could they possibly do that?

168

Yue Yi, Guan Zhong and Zhu Geliang were invincible in attack and defence. If they had not known the heaven and earth, how could they possibly do that?

169

Wang Meng helped stablise Qin and Xie An defended Jin; if they had not appointed qualified generals and talents and strengthened the troops, how could they possibly do that?

170

Therefore, in order to study the art of war, you must first learn from the third level to the second and then from the second to the first.

171

Then you will progress from the elementary to the profound.

172

Otherwise, you will learn nothing but empty talks and parroting.

173

That is not the right thing to do."

174

Emperor Taizong said: "Taoists believe that it is forbidden to have men as generals for three generations in the same family.

175

The art of war cannot be taught without consideration.

176

You should impart the knowledge in a serious and cautious manner."

177

Li Jing bowed and left.

178

He instructed Li Ji with all his military classics.